UNDERWATER WORLD

TAMARA MACFARLANE

Illustrated by Alessandra Fusi

Contents

The land beneath the waves

Stop for a minute and imagine that in one great whoosh, every drop of water from the seas and oceans suddenly shot into the air, revealing everything that was underneath.

When you think of the planet this way, it is easier to imagine the extraordinary things that were previously hidden. In an instant, we could see a miracle of wonders revealed. Creatures from the deepest of deep, so strange that you can barely believe they exist, glowing microbes, sea plants that breathe out clean air for us, coral, seagrass, mangroves, shipwrecks, sunken cities, and much more.

And these are just the things we know about. More than 80 percent of the oceans are unexplored, meaning we know more about the surface of the moon than about the oceans that cover our own planet. So what lurks under the surface? Turn the pages and see...

MYTHS AND MONSTERS

From merpeople and sea serpents, to kelpies and the mighty kraken, cultures all across the world have their share of water-based myths and legends. Turn the pages to meet some of these mythical beasts and magical creatures.

Wave goddesses
SCANDINAVIA

Mishipeshu
NORTH AMERICA

Kelpie
SCOTLAND

Hydra
EUROPE

Encantado
SOUTH AMERICA

Mami Wata
AFRICA

Legendary creatures

I n uncharted waters, where we are yet to visit, mysterious creatures are said to roam and swim through secret lands. Are these myths and legends the work of human imagination, or are they as real as you are? Decide for yourself...

Yacumama
SOUTH AMERICA

Iku-Turso
FINLAND

Dragon kings
CHINA

Leviathan
MIDDLE EAST

Zaratan
MIDDLE EAST

N

Bunyip
AUSTRALIA

Neptune
The Roman god of water is known to have a stormy temper strong enough to create earthquakes.

Kamohoalii
This shape-shifting Hawaiian shark god can transform into any fish, and is said to guide lost ships back to safety.

Water deities

Worshipped by cultures all around the world, water goddesses and gods have long ruled the waves of mythology.

Ryujin
Ryujin is a Japanese dragon king who rules the tides from a beautiful underwater palace. He represents both the dangers and the magnificence of the sea.

Mami Wata
Mami Wata (Mother Water) is celebrated across Africa and many communities across the Americas. Like water, she can be both life giving and dangerous.

Alignak

God of the moon and weather in Inuit mythology, Alignak is responsible for producing waves, earthquakes, comets, and eclipses.

Rainbow serpent

This Aboriginal god is usually linked with water and rain. The serpent's importance reflects the importance of water in human life.

Chalchiuhtlicue

Chalchiuhtlicue's name means "she of the jade skirt." She is protector of Earth's water, and is one of the most important Aztec goddesses.

Varuna

This Hindu deity is the human form of the sky, clouds, water, rivers, and ocean animals.

Ran

This Norse goddess of the sea is usually shown with a net, which she uses to catch sea goers.

Namaka

The Hawaiian water goddess Namaka is the sister of Kamahoalii. She has the power to create tidal waves.

Nine wave goddesses

According to Norse mythology, each of these nine goddesses personifies a different aspect of a wave, such as movement or foam.

HIMINGLÆVA
Heaven-Clear
(a reference to the
transparency of water).

DÚFA
Dipping Wave.

BLÓÐUGHADDA
Bloody-Hair (a reference
to red sea foam).

HEFRING
Rising Wave.

UÐR
Frothing Wave.

HRÖNN
Welling Wave.

BYLGJA
Billowing Wave.

DRÖFN
Foam-Fleck.

KÓLGA
Cool Wave.

Five dragon kings

In Chinese mythology, the five dragon kings are said to rule the seas, led by Longwang, the Dragon King.

LONGWANG, THE DRAGON KING

Longwang is a shape-shifter who can appear in dragon form or as a powerful human warrior. He is the ruler of all water, and has four brothers who rule the waters to the north, south, east, and west...

AO GUANG, THE AZURE DRAGON

This dragon king is the lord of the east and of spring. He controls the waters of the East China Sea.

AO RUN, THE WHITE DRAGON

Ao Run represents the west and fall. He is the lord of Qinghai Lake.

AO SHUN, THE BLACK DRAGON

Ao Shun is the lord of winter. He rules over the northern waters.

AO QIN, THE RED DRAGON

This dragon king rules over the South China Sea. He is also the lord of summer.

La Pincoya
The Chilean legend of La Pincoya tells the tale of a woman who drinks a potion that turns her into water, and is poured into the sea.

Jiaoren
In the seas and lakes of China, Jiaoren weaves dragon yarn into fabric and sews pearls, formed from their tears into great works of art.

Pania
In Maori legend, Pania fell in love with the son of a Maori chief. She divided her time between living on land with him, and in the sea with her merpeople.

Merpeople

Swimming through folktales around the world, these creatures have inspired legendary stories.

Siyokoy
The terrifying Siyokoy swims in waters around the Philippines eating any humans who might be a danger to the ocean or its creatures.

Sirena
Sirena is said to have a voice so beautiful, sailors will follow it anywhere. She is known to lure them into rocks and sink their ships.

Melusine
A figure from French folklore, Melusine was cursed to become half fish every Saturday.

Matsya
The Hindu god Vishnu appeared in the form of a merman named Matsya in order to save the world from devastating floods.

Oshun
The daughter of a sea god of the Yoruba people in West Africa, Oshun created water, and with that water came all life on Earth.

Ningyo
Ningyo are creatures that resemble fish more closely than humans. They appear in Japanese legend with sharp claws and hideous faces.

Chitapo
Lurking in African waters, the chitapo are evil water spirits who lure humans into the water and swallow them up.

Sedna
In Inuit mythology, Sedna is a goddess of the sea. After falling into the water during a storm and losing her fingers, they regrew as seals, whales, and walruses.

The Sea-foam

Based on Celtic myths and legends of kelpies.

"Promise me you won't go near the water," Aidan's mother called as she left the house. It was the first time Aidan had stayed home alone. His mind was full of adventures.

Aidan closed the door and looked outside, trying to decide which adventure to have first. Should he take the boat out, swim in the loch, or paint?

Aidan wondered why everything he wanted to do was near water. Perhaps his mom meant not to go **into** the water, rather than not to go near it. That must be it. He decided to go painting, and set off.

Jumping onto his favorite rock, Aidan dipped his brush into a tide pool and stared at the water. He wanted to paint every shade of blue, green, and black he could see. He ran strokes of white-blue across the paper, reflecting the foam riding on the waves, then, blue-black paint for the deeper water.

Aidan stared into the loch. The harder he stared, the stranger it looked, until it suddenly began to spin like a whirlpool. Desperate to capture the spiraling colors, Aidan leaned forward. In a giant whoosh, the water rose up and sucked him in.

For a moment, there was nothing but darkness and falling.

Aidan was about to gasp for air, but the water slowed and he rose toward the light. Bursting through the surface, he breathed in. The foam swirled and lifted him up. The feeling reminded him of something from his bedtime stories.

Suddenly, the foam took on a familiar form and reared up above the sea with Aidan on its back. It was a kelpie! The horselike creature had a frothing mane of foam, eyes as black as eels, and a shimmering pearl coat.

Aidan knew the kelpie stories. They were shape-shifting monsters who were said to steal children from the water's edge, never to return again.

The kelpie leapt into the air. Aidan reached his arms around its neck, and found a pair of seaweed reins. He gripped them so tightly that his knuckles glowed white as they dove into the loch.

With his face pressed into the mane of foam, Aidan found just enough air to breathe. The kelpie cantered on, until they were far from land.

Aidan heard a crying sound. Was it the cries of the children who'd been taken? Was he about to join them? The cries became louder and Aidan's heart beat faster. He closed his eyes, but they were jolted open as something slimy swept across his face. The cries were almost deafening now.

In the gloom of the deep, Aidan saw a fishing net and at least a hundred trapped, crying seals.

He had to help. Aidan pulled the reins and steered the kelpie to the seabed. He grabbed a sharp shell and used it to cut a hole in the net. As they swam away to freedom, each seal brushed Aidan with their nose to thank him. He gathered up the net and hauled it onto the kelpie's back.

Perhaps kelpies are actually protecting sea creatures from humans, he thought.

The kelpie neighed its thanks, galloping Aidan back to land. Aidan called goodbye as his new friend dissolved into the water, leaving nothing but foam and seaweed behind.

"What a beautiful painting," Aidan's mother exclaimed as she made him dinner that evening. "You have such a wonderful imagination, painting a kelpie, just like the ones in the stories. I just hope you never see a real one. Although, I can't imagine they are as monstrous as people say!"

18

Kelpie

Riding the waves, this malevolent spirit
from Scottish folklore can take different
forms, but most often appears as
a horselike creature.

APPEARANCE
This tricky shape-shifter appears as
a pony on land, but once in the water,
its hooves reverse and it becomes
a monster covered in seaweed.

DWELLING
The kelpie haunts lochs and
other bodies of water.

POWERS AND TRAITS
• Shape-shifting
• A sticky hide that traps prey

Akkorokamui
Creeping from the pages of
Japanese folklore, this colossal
octopus-like creature is said to
glow red, like a setting sun.

Bakunawa
Slashing its looped tail through the water,
this fearsome water serpent from the
Philippines is capable of swallowing the
moon and causing natural disasters.

Sea monsters

Almost every culture tells tales of incredible
creatures that take a number of forms.
Are they friend or foe? You decide...

Mokèlé-Mbèmbé
Haunting the Congo River, this long-necked
monster whose name means "one who stops
the flow of waters" is capable of swallowing
elephants that come to the water to drink.

Zaratan
Zaratan is a huge turtle that is often mistaken for an island. It is said to sleep for ten years at a time.

Leviathan
Also known as Hellmouth, Leviathan is an evil, envious sea serpent that swallows ships and creates chaos.

Mishipeshu
Described as a cross between a cat and a dragon, this Native American water panther appears in a number of legends.

Qalupalik
The claws of this scaly Inuit monster lurk just under the icy water, waiting to catch any child who wanders too close.

Ahuizotl
In Aztec legend, Ahuizotl resembles a dog that wields a humanlike hand at the end of its tail. It sometimes cries like a child to trap humans.

Yacumama
This enormous water serpent and its terrifying jaws slither along the Amazon River looking for humans to prey on.

Nessie

With more than 1,000 reported sightings, the debate continues as to whether this creature really exists and actually swims up and down Loch Ness, Scotland.

Hydra

This monster of Greek mythology is said to lurk by the gates of Hades. Each time one of its heads is cut off, two grow back, making it almost impossible to destroy.

Ponaturi

In Maori mythology, the Ponaturi live under the sea during the day to avoid the sunlight, which can kill them. At night, they come up to the shore to sleep.

Tumu-Ra-i-Fuena

This creature can be found in Tahitian legends. It is so huge it can grip the Earth and the Moon in its tentacles at the same time.

Bunyip

This monster from Aboriginal folklore lives in swamps and lagoons. It is known for making roaring noises, and has been said to eat humans.

Hippocampus
This striking seahorse with its half-horse, half-fish body exists in many legends worldwide.

Encantado
Musical and party loving, this Brazilian dolphinlike creature can shape-shift into human form, but can always be identified by the blow hole on top of its head.

Nuckelavee
Also known as the "Devil of the Sea," the Nuckelavee was said to terrify the islanders of northern Scotland.

Nykr
These Scandinavian water spirits lure humans to the water with their beautiful violin playing.

Selkie
On land, a selkie sheds its sealskin to reveal a human form. If the skin is lost or stolen, the selkie is unable to return to the sea until it is found.

The kraken

Formed from the nightmares of every daring
seafarer, this terrifying tentacled creature
lurks in the depths, waiting…

THE LEGEND

A swarm of fish appears, so vast that the whole sea darkens. The tip of a fanged tentacle reaches through the surface. Then, in a sudden surge, the kraken breaks through in a fountain of sea foam, writhing in all its horrifying glory. In less time than it takes for your heart to stop beating in terror, your ship is engulfed, and you are pulled beneath the surface to your doom.

FROM FANTASY TO FACT

The descriptions from fishermen were so vivid and consistent that it was believed for a long time that the kraken was a real creature. We now think that the kraken is most likely to have come about from the imaginations of people finding the rotten remains of colossal squid washed up on beaches, or sightings of giant squid out at sea in the cold Nordic waters where the original kraken legend emerged.

Unu Pachakuti

The Inca god, Viracocha, is said to have once created a race of giants. The giants, however, wouldn't obey him so he destroyed them with a mighty flood called Unu Pachakuti, and created human beings instead.

Zeus and the great flood

When the Greek god Zeus became angry at the behavior of humans, he punished them by flooding the Earth. Only two people survived, who created more humans by throwing stones over their shoulders.

Flood myths

Flood myths are found in cultures from all over the world. Many of the stories are similar, and involve themes of rebirth and starting fresh.

The Gilgamesh flood myth

Considered to be the oldest flood myth, this is one of the first recorded stories in the history of literature, and is similar to the biblical story of Noah's Ark.

Waynaboozhoo and the great flood

In this Native American legend, Waynaboozhoo is the only survivor of a great flood, and must rebuild the Earth by placing mud onto a snapping turtle and letting it grow.

Ymir

In Norse myth, when Odin killed the frost giant, Ymir, his blood flowed so heavily it caused a huge flood. A new world then formed from Ymir's body—his blood became the rivers, his hair the trees, and his bones the mountains.

Cameroonian legend

This story from Cameroon involves a young girl who was grinding flour and allowed a hungry goat to feast on it. To thank her, the goat warned her that a flood was coming. The girl grabbed her brother and fled to safety.

Manu and Matsya

According to Hindu legend, the god Vishnu warned King Manu of a great upcoming flood and sent him a boat. Once the flooding started, Vishnu took the form of Matsya, a golden fish with a horn. Manu then tied Matsya to the side of the boat so that he could lead him to safety.

Yu the Great

Ancient China was once battered by terrible floods. After years of work, Yu the Great is said to have invented ways to move the overflowing water from the rivers onto the fields, turning the banks of the yellow river into places where culture could thrive.

Noah's Ark

In this story from the Bible, God became angry at humans, so He sent a great flood to wipe them out. He tasked Noah—a man deemed good—and his family to build an ark to carry two of each animal to safety.

Atlantis

A mythical land of legend.

Atlantis is the most famous of the mythical underwater lands. It was said to have been a vast island kingdom that was sunk by an earthquake.

Poseidon

Atlantis?

ATLANTIC OCEAN

The son of the Greek god Poseidon, Atlas, who is famous in mythology for holding up the Earth, was—according to Plato—the first king of Atlantis.

Atlas

PLATO'S STORY
The Greek philosopher Plato described the city of Atlantis as an island sparkling with gold and silver that is surrounded by three rings of alternating water and land.

THE SEARCH FOR ANSWERS
Satellite imagery has found a site with circular land and water structures similar to those Plato described off the coast of Spain, but the area cannot be excavated.

FACT OR FICTION?
Most people now think that Plato's legendary island only existed in his story, but divers, archaeologists, and historians continue to search for it, just in case!

SUNKEN CITIES AND LOST LANDS

Sometimes, almost perfectly preserved on the seafloor, lie whole villages, towns, and cities. Where they once bustled with human life, fish now swim through the arches, stream through the doorways, and circle up around long forgotten statues.

Doggerland
BRITAIN

Cantre'r
Gwaelod
WALES

Pavlopetri
GREECE

Thônis-Heracleion
EGYPT

Port Royal
JAMAICA

N

Shi Cheng City
CHINA

Yonaguni Pyramids
JAPAN

Atlit-Yam
ISRAEL

Nan Madol
FEDERATED STATES OF MICRONESIA

Sunken cities

S unken cities don't only exist in fiction like Atlantis.
There are many real places around the globe that have
been washed under the waves. Each city has its own
fascinating history of how it ended up under the water.
Was it the workings of a natural disaster, or was it built
that way by humankind?

The Floodgates and the Forgotten Forest

A legend based on stories of the
submerged kingdom of Cantre'r Gwaelod, Wales.

Born of a tree father and a mother sea spirit, Meriarid was gifted with the power to hear the Earth as it talked.

The king and queen searched far and wide for someone with this power. They needed someone to warn them of floods so they could protect their precious kingdom.

Word reached them through the forest, of Meriarid, this special girl, who could feel the tides in her veins and tell of the winds. They sent her a message requesting that she come to their palace.

Meriarid was a quiet girl from a different kind of kingdom, one of birds and streams and pebbles. She sent a polite reply to say thank you for the invitation, but she could not leave her forest alone.

In frustration, the king and queen rode into the depths of the forest to find Meriarid, and requested that she come down from the treetops.

Effortlessly hopping from branch to branch, Meriarid descended until she perched on a branch just above them.

"We need you to guard the floodgates that keep the sea from our shores," said the king. "You have the power to know when a storm is coming, so we can close them in time," added the queen.

"But I do not want to leave my forest," Meriarid said.

"Help us, or we will chop down one tree every day, until there is no forest left," said the king. "Come before sunrise tomorrow, or we will send out the woodcutter," he added, before rearing his horse and turning toward his palace.

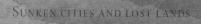

Left with no choice, Meriarid folded up her few possessions in a large leaf, and reluctantly began her journey across the treetops toward the palace and the floodgates.

For almost ten years, Meriarid protected the people, the town, and the palace from floods. Each time her fingertips twitched, she leapt down to warn the guards to close the gates, and each time they kept out the waves successfully.

But one evening, something felt very different.

The twitching in Meriarid's fingers was painful, as though she was being warned of something worse. She felt a chill run down her spine and she couldn't stop shivering. "I must warn the guards that a huge storm is coming!"

Meriarid ran down to the gates, but the guards were not there.

Up on the hill, the king and queen were throwing a huge banquet, and the two guards were feasting, drinking, and laughing. Loud music was playing, and nobody heard Meriarid's cries for help.

When the storm began, the twitching in Meriarid's fingers became sharper, and the chill froze her until she could hardly move. Still, she called for help.

Finally, a local family heard her cries and sent their daughter to the palace with a message for help.

Together with the rest of the family, Meriarid tried to close the floodgates. They pulled and pulled to try to shut out the stormy waves, but the gates were locked and only the guards had the keys.

Realizing it was hopeless, Meriarid and the kind family called to all the townspeople to run for the hills, and stayed to help those who couldn't make it on their own.

They ran from house to house to make sure nobody was left behind, even as the water rushed in.

Meriarid and the kind family's bravery saved the people of the town, and the daughter's message saved the people of the palace. It was too late, however, to save the forest. The guards had run off with the keys to save themselves and left the forest to flood.

It is said that to this day, Meriarid sits on the shore staring out to sea, watching over her forgotten forest, which now lies buried beneath the waves.

Cantre'r Gwaelod

Myth or reality? The uncovering of a forgotten forest.

Cantre'r Gwaelod is a mythical sunken kingdom that appears in Welsh folklore, and is sometimes called the "Welsh Atlantis." Many of the legends involve a great forest. Are the stories from myth true, or just fantasy? A recent discovery of a submerged forest may hold some clues...

CAUSE OF SUBMERSION

In 2019, a huge storm unearthed a previously lost forest that is thought to have been buried by rising sea levels.

AMAZING DISCOVERIES

The rediscovery of this 5,500 year old site turned myth into possibility by confirming that a forest had once existed in the area. Evidence for whether the events of those legends are also true, however, has yet to be found.

Yonaguni Pyramids

Built by nature or a man-made mountain?

This vast underwater rock formation, found off the coast of Yonaguni Island, Japan, appears to be a set of huge stone steps. Discovered by scuba divers in 1986, archaeologists date the rock formation to be over 2,000 years old.

CAUSE OF SUBMERSION

The specific cause is unknown, but rising sea levels, a tsunami, or an earthquake are the most likely causes.

AMAZING DISCOVERIES

Shapes of animals, including two turtles, appear to be set into the stone. These may link the pyramids to the lost land of Mu from Japanese folklore, said to be guarded by turtles. To this day, the origins of the pyramids remain a mystery, since scientists and archaeologists cannot agree on whether they are a man-made underwater city that once housed an ancient civilization, or a rock formation shaped by nature.

Thônis-Heracleion

An ancient civilization preserved in time.

This ancient city was built on a marshland of lakes, sandbanks, and islands where the Nile River met the Mediterranean Sea. It was an important Egyptian trading hub, and one of the greatest port cities in the world until it was submerged in the 8th century. It lay undisturbed for more than 1,000 years before being rediscovered by marine archaeologists in the early 2000s.

CAUSE OF SUBMERSION

A series of natural disasters including an earthquake and a tsunami liquefied the land beneath the city, causing it to sink.

AMAZING DISCOVERIES

The exploration of this vast site revealed the city as a place where Greek and Egyptian people mixed. This can be seen in extraordinary artwork, including statues originating from both cultures.

A MYSTERY SOLVED

Historians used to think Thônis and Heracleion were two different lost cities, but a stone tablet discovered on this site showed that Thônis was the Egyptian name and Heracleion was the Greek name for the same city. This incredible site is home to countless treasures, and is still being explored today.

Port Royal

A sunken port of pirates, privateers, and treasure.

Located on the coast of Jamaica and known as "the wickedest city on Earth," Port Royal was an important trading hub in the 17th century. Its location as a natural harbor made it an excellent center for traders, sailors, pirates, and privateers.

CAUSE OF SUBMERSION

In 1692, an earthquake hit the area, sinking two thirds of the city. The remaining third is now a small fishing village.

AMAZING DISCOVERIES

Port Royal's pirate history was legendary, but the really exceptional thing about the city was that it sank in just minutes. Because of this, it remains almost perfectly preserved, and is now an important archaeological site.

Shi Cheng City

A perfectly preserved underwater city.

Located beneath the waters of Qiandao Lake, China, Shi Cheng City (also known as Lion City), was part of an important empire between 25-200 CE. During this time, it was one of the most powerful cities of ancient China.

CAUSE OF SUBMERSION

In 1959, the government flooded the area so they could create a dam and generate hydroelectricity.

AMAZING DISCOVERIES

In 2014, it was found that despite over 50 years underwater, the city remained in great condition.

Nan Madol

The only remaining ancient city built on coral reefs.

Nan Madol on Pohnpei Island, Federated States of Micronesia, appears to float on the water. It was built on coral reefs, and inhabited for around 500 years from 1200 CE to 1700 CE. It was a major political and spiritual place for native Pohnpeians, and had forts, places of worship, markets, and a royal enclave.

CAUSE OF SUBMERSION
The remains of Nan Madol still stand above water as an example of the amazingly advanced marine building skills of the Pohnpei people.

AMAZING DISCOVERIES
The building skill used to create Nan Madol was so advanced that archaeologists are still not sure how the large stones were moved into place, or how the foundations have stayed together for so long.

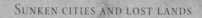

Doggerland

UK

Among the discoveries from the area are wooden totem-pole-like posts.

Mainland Europe

Doggerland

A Stone Age land lost to rising sea levels.

Thousands of years ago, what is now the UK was firmly attached to the rest of Europe by a piece of land known as Doggerland. Today, Doggerland sits beneath the North Sea.

CAUSE OF SUBMERSION

More than 8,000 years ago, a warming climate caused the release of water from glaciers, turning Doggerland into an island. Later, a colossal underwater landslide off the coast of Norway caused a tsunami which led to additional flooding. It is thought that further warming then brought more gradual floods that eventually cut Britain off completely from the rest of Europe.

AMAZING DISCOVERIES

In the early 20th century, archaeologists recovered remains of animals from Doggerland, including lions, hippos, and mammoths, as well as many human tools and remains.

A 50,000-year-old flint tool was discovered in the area in 2016.

Pavlopetri

The oldest underwater city in the world.

The ancient city of Pavlopetri, discovered off the coast of Greece in 1967, is thought to be the oldest underwater city in the world. It was an important port which lay forgotten under the waves for more than 3,000 years. It had carefully planned roads, temples, and homes that put it ahead of its time in human history.

CAUSE OF SUBMERSION

The first of three massive earthquakes that hit the area is believed to have completely submerged the town sometime around 1000 BCE.

AMAZING DISCOVERIES

Although Pavlopetri has eroded after thousands of years underwater, the city is fairly well preserved, with full buildings, roads, and temples that can be explored by divers looking for Bronze Age objects.

Atlit-Yam

An abandoned settlement deep under the seabed.

This ancient village in the Mediterranean Sea off the coast of Israel is so well preserved beneath the seabed that human skeletons lie unmoved in their graves, and insects are preserved in food containers. Although there is no evidence of roads, stone houses with paved floors and fireplaces have been found.

CAUSE OF SUBMERSION

Around 8,500 years ago, part of Mount Etna collapsed, causing a huge tsunami that engulfed and submerged the village.

AMAZING DISCOVERIES

The site lay buried for nearly 9,000 years until a marine archaeologist surveying the area for shipwrecks discovered some ancient remains that had been exposed by sand quarrying in the area. The site is home to the oldest man-made well that has ever been uncovered by archaeologists.

MARINE MYSTERIES

There are so many mysteries above and below the ocean's surface. Many of them will be solved as we continue to explore the ocean floor, but many mysteries, that nobody has been able to explain, remain.

Ghost ships

Haunted and mysterious vessels have long been a fixture of legends and folktales. But the term "ghost ships" also refers to real ships found sailing without a living crew aboard.

Throughout maritime history, crews have abandoned their ships or simply disappeared, often in unknown circumstances, leaving ships to sail wherever the waves carry them. Despite several investigations, many of these cases remain unsolved.

HMS RESOLUTE

HMS Resolute was one of several British ships sent on an expedition to rescue the Arctic explorer, John Franklin. It became trapped in ice, however, and had to be abandoned. *HMS Resolute* later drifted for about 1,200 miles (1,900 km) across the icy seas until it was discovered by a merchant ship off the coast of Baffin Island, Canada.

MARY CELESTE

In 1872, *Mary Celeste* set sail from New York, US on its way to Genoa, Italy. It was spotted off the coast of the Azores Islands in the Atlantic Ocean by a merchant ship whose captain was alarmed by its erratic passage. *Mary Celeste* was missing a life boat, but was otherwise totally seaworthy—with no explanation as to why it had been abandoned. There were no known survivors.

SS BAYCHIMO

In 1931, **SS *Baychimo*** became trapped in the Arctic ice. Half of the crew was rescued by airplane, and half stayed to wait out the winter until the ship was freed. A storm damaged the ship more, however, so the crew left it to the elements believing it would be taken by the sea within a week. **SS *Baychimo*** drifted around the Arctic waters for at least 39 years. It was last sighted in 1969.

Over the years, there have been several attempts to salvage SS *Baychimo*, but none have been successful.

SV GOVERNOR PARR

On the way to Buenos Aires, Argentina, **SV *Governor Parr*** suffered significant damage in a storm. The crew escaped safely, and several attempts were made to tow the derelict ship to shore, or to destroy it so it wouldn't be a danger to other ships, but they all failed. For many years, the ship was sighted across different parts of the Atlantic Ocean. Nobody knows where the ship is now, or how it survived for so long without a crew.

CARROLL A. DEERING

Carroll A. Deering was found sailing off the coast of North Carolina, US with no crew. Its final voyage was investigated by the US government, since it was one of several ships that disappeared in a short space of time. Despite the investigations as to why the ship was abandoned, it remains a mystery, but piracy is the most likely explanation.

Phantom vessels

Many mysterious ghostly ships have been seen at sea. What became of them?

THE FLYING DUTCHMAN

In 1641, Captain Hendrick Van der Decken, otherwise known as "The Dutchman," sailed his ship straight into a storm and sank it off the Cape of Good Hope, South Africa. It is said that the ship is cursed to sail the seas for eternity, and to this day, sailors still report sightings of it.

LADY LOVIBOND

On February 13th, 1748, the crew of *Lady Lovibond* was celebrating a wedding. All were happy except for the ship's first mate, who was secretly in love with the bride. His anger and jealousy caused him to deliberately sail the ship into a sandbank off the coast of the UK, sinking it. Ever since, vessels in the area have reported sightings of it.

EL CALEUCHE

Legend says that *El Caleuche* appears each evening off the coast of Chile carrying the spirits of people who have died at sea. It is said that the beautiful ship sails around catching these souls, and that they appear aboard full of cheer, surrounded by lights.

THE FIRESHIP OF CHALEUR BAY

It is said that tens of thousands of people have seen a mysterious ship in Chaleur Bay, Canada. It is possible that the apparition is actually the result of a natural phenomena caused by marine life, but locals are convinced it is a phantom vessel.

YOUNG TEAZER

Young Teazer is a popular Canadian phantom ship story. In 1813, after stealing from another ship, she was fired upon. Desperate not to have the ship boarded by another crew, the captain lit the onboard supply of gunpowder, and the ship exploded. For years, witnesses reported seeing a glowing ship floating in the bay. This became known as the "Teazer Light."

RMS Rhone
Divers near this shipwreck in the Caribbean have reported hearing screams and seeing people swimming toward the surface. But when the divers approached them to help, the swimmers disappeared.

Haunted wrecks

In addition to tales of ghost ships and phantom vessels, there are also reports of haunted wrecks that litter the ocean floor.

SS Andrea Doria
Divers have reported seeing strange shadows gathered around this shipwreck off the coast of Italy.

SS Thistlegorm
SS Thistlegorm sunk in the Red Sea during World War II. Since then, the sound of engines and sightings of ghostly figures have frequently been reported nearby.

Messerschmitt ME Gigant
Sightings of crew members from this wrecked airplane off the coast of Italy have been reported by a number of divers. They claim that when they approach them, the figures disappear.

Le Griffon
Sailors speak of a ghostly ship coming toward them in the location of this wreck in Lake Michigan, US. Divers have also reported seeing a vast ship above them, that vanishes when they go to the surface.

The Bermuda Triangle

An unsolved oceanic mystery.

The Bermuda Triangle sits at the tip of Florida, US between the three points of Miami, Bermuda, and Puerto Rico. It has become legendary because a large number of planes and boats that have passed through have vanished without a trace. Despite numerous investigations and many theories—from extraterrestrial interference to unique weather systems, a significant number of these mysterious incidents remain unsolved.

COLUMBUS'S CROSSING

During his first voyage to the Americas, Christopher Columbus recorded seeing a great flame crashing into the sea in the area now referred to as the Bermuda Triangle. He also reported strange compass readings.

FLIGHT 19

On one fateful day in 1945, five US Navy bombers carrying 14 crew members took off from Florida on a practice mission. Shortly into the flight, the compasses on the leader's plane stopped working properly. They flew around without direction until they ran out of fuel. The crew and planes were never found, and no evidence as to what happened has been recovered.

Florida

Bermuda

Miami

Bermuda Triangle

Puerto Rico

Timeline

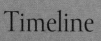

1881: The Ellen Austin's crew vanishes.

1945: The planes and crew from Flight 19 vanish.

1492: Christopher Columbus reports flames crashing into the sea.

1921: The Carroll A. Deering's crew vanishes.

Japan

The Devil's Sea

A small area in the Bermuda Triangle is one of the few places on Earth where true North and Magnetic North line up (which can cause compasses to malfunction). This also occurs in an area off the coast of Japan known as the Devil's Sea, which also has a reputation for strange occurences.

Underwater trenches

Some of the deepest underwater trenches in the world are located within the Bermuda Triangle. One theory about why wrecked planes and ships appear to vanish is that they sink to the bottom of one of these trenches.

The Gulf Stream

Another possible explanation for the mysteries, is that the Gulf Stream—a strong ocean current that can cause sudden weather changes—passes through the Bermuda Triangle.

1968: The submarine USS Scorpion sinks.

1976: The cargo ship Sylvia L. Ossa and its crew disappear.

1980: The SS Poet and all its crew disappear.

2017: A small private airplane vanishes without a trace.

DEEP-SEA DISCOVERIES

The mysteries of the ocean aren't just limited to myths and monsters. From ancient shipwrecks and natural phenomena to unusual creatures from the deep, there are plenty of real mysteries out there being investigated by ocean experts.

Stranger than fiction

While the creatures of myth and legend often defy belief, the ocean depths are also home to some equally strange, but very real animals.

Goblin shark
This extraordinary looking shark has an extendable jaw that it thrusts out of its own mouth to catch prey.

Pointy-nosed blue chimaera
These elusive and mysterious sharks are also known as ghost sharks, and live deeper than the sun's rays can reach.

Anglerfish
These deep-sea fish lure their prey with special rods above their mouths that glow in the dark. They can also swallow prey up to twice their own size.

Vampire squid
With the ability to throw a camouflaging cape of tentacles over itself while releasing a glowing substance to confuse predators, the vampire squid is a truly talented creature.

Colossal squid
The largest invertebrate in the world, this massive squid has tentacles laced with suckers and hooks, and has the largest eyes of any creature on Earth.

Faceless cusk eel
This eel has tiny eyes, so it relies instead on special organs in its head to help it figure out its surroundings.

Flapjack octopus
This small, round, spongy octopus can transform its transparent reddish body into a flat shape in the blink of an eye.

Underwater phenomena

Under the surface of the ocean, extraordinary things
occur unseen, including erupting volcanoes,
flowing rivers, and tumbling waterfalls.

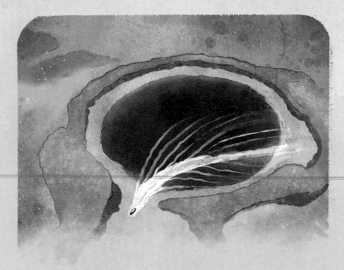

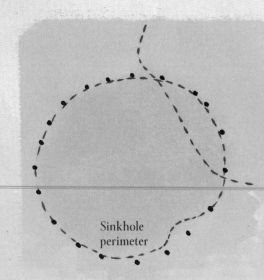

Blue holes
Blue holes are underwater sinkholes. The most famous
is the Great Blue Hole in Belize, which is about 1000 ft
(300 m) across and 400 ft (125 m) deep.

To learn more about the Great Blue Hole, scientists used
special cameras and sonar to map its perimeter, then went
on submarine expeditions to reach the bottom.

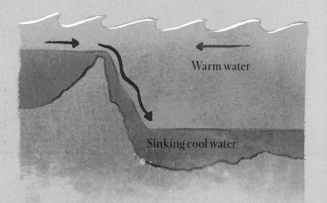

Underwater waterfalls
The largest waterfall in the world is actually
in the ocean, between Greenland and Iceland.
It cascades for more than 11,500 ft (3,500 m)!

When cold and warm water meet in the ocean, the
cold water sinks. If this cold water flows over an
underwater cliff edge, it sinks beneath the
warmer water, forming a waterfall.

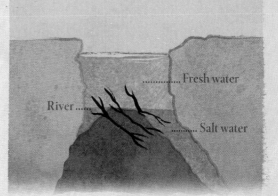

Underwater rivers

In some rare places where salt and fresh water mix in just the right way, it creates a river of flowing water deep under the surface.

Underwater rivers occur in places where fresh and salt water meet. The different density levels in the water, causes them to layer, creating the effect shown above.

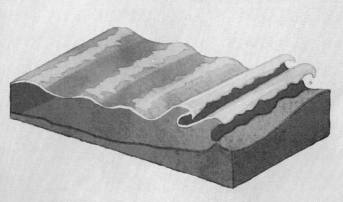

Tsunamis

Tsunamis are enormous waves. In 1958, one of the largest tsunamis ever recorded washed over Lituya Bay, Alaska. The wave reached heights of more than 1,640 ft (500 m).

Tsunamis are a series of waves that are created when water is displaced by earthquakes, volcanic eruptions, or landslides that occur under the ocean.

Underwater volcanoes

There are an estimated 1 million underwater volcanoes in the world. A number of key islands, including the Hawaiian Islands were formed from underwater volcanic eruptions.

Underwater volcanoes form when movement in the Earth's crust allows magma to escape as lava. When the lava cools and hardens, new land is formed.

Color striped icebergs
Over two thirds of Earth's fresh water is contained in glaciers. These can appear to have blue stripes when different layers freeze at different speeds.

Natural phenomena

Our oceans and seas have inspired libraries full of fantasy, myth, and legend, but few are as strange as the reality of natural water phenomena.

Clashing waters
Off the coast of Denmark, the North Sea and the Baltic Sea meet from opposite directions. Because the North Sea is saltier and colder than the Baltic Sea, the two do not mix.

Rogue waves
Sometimes, and without known reason, gigantic waves appear in the middle of the ocean. They can be 40 ft (12 m) high, and powerful enough to destroy ships and oil rigs.

Brinicles

Brinicles are huge icicles formed underwater in the Antarctic Ocean. When they touch the ocean floor, they freeze and kill almost anything they come into contact with.

Frost flowers

Thin layers of ice on the ocean take in surrounding water and grow into petal-like structures. These frosty flowers then sit on the surface as a home to marine bacteria.

Whirlpools

Whirlpools are rotating bodies of water currents flowing in different directions. Large, powerful whirlpools are called maelstroms, and are strong enough to pull boats into them.

Extraordinary nature

The natural world is full of wonders, but it also plays a vital role in our protection. This is why it's so important that we do everything we can to protect it, too.

Mangroves
Mangrove forests rise from the water as a tangle of clustered roots. This root system can slow the impact of tidal waves, protecting the coastline from flooding and erosion.

Seagrass

Underwater seagrass beds disrupt sediment moving with the tides. This creates a greater living environment for marine life. They also add oxygen to their surroundings and provide food for many aquatic creatures.

Coral

Coral reefs are made from the skeletal remains of sea creatures called polyps. Not only are coral reefs one of the most diverse ecosystems on Earth, they can also absorb wave energy and protect the coastline.

Design a deep-sea map

Oceanographers spend their lives mapping the ocean floors. Can you create your own imaginary map and plot it out using the ideas on this page? Use the grid on the right page for inspiration.

What treasure can be found using your map? Pirate gold, a lost land, haunted shipwrecks, the discovery of a natural phenomena, or the rarest deep-sea creature on the planet? Imagine what incredible discoveries your map may lead you to. The choice is yours...

POSSIBLE THINGS TO INCLUDE:

• A key—create a key of symbols to show what each of the things on your map mean.

• A compass—to show which way is north. Useful for any map!

• Any information that an explorer with your map may need to know about overcoming obstacles on the way. For example, is the treasure protected by 100 electric eels? Perhaps these eels are distracted by bright lights so you need to take an underwater flashlight and shine the light away from you. Use your imagination!

• Information about the surrounding areas—is there a blue hole nearby that you need to dive into in order to reach the secret spot? Are the currents around it too strong?

Key

Coral reef

Haunted shipwreck

Wrecked airplane

Underwater waterfall

Seagrass

Mangrove forest

Abandoned statue

Sandbank

Coastline

Underwater museum

Create your own deep-sea creature

Deep-sea creatures are some of the most amazing and unusual animals in the world, and often have incredible abilities or features. Why not invent your own deep-sea creature by mixing and matching the options below?

Body type

Flat
Having a flat body helps fish hide. Flat fish can lie sideways on the seabed to blend in.

Torpedo
Torpedo-shaped bodies allow fish to swim through the water quickly.

Snake
A snake-like body allows sea creatures to sneak up on prey by sliding through narrow passages.

Blob
Blob fish are mostly made of a jellylike substance, and float around with the tides.

Features

 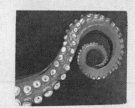  

Fins
Like oars and propellers on a boat, fish use fins to help steer through the water.

Tentacles
Squid and octopuses use their tentacles to grab prey. Tentacles also help propel them through the water.

Tails
Streamlined and full of muscle, tails are used to help fish swim long distances.

Limbs
Some creatures, such as starfish, have limbs. Some starfish species can have as many as 40.

Defense mechanisms

Inflation
Blowfish puff up to twice their original size by sucking in water in order to discourage predators.

Ink
When threatened, squid release ink into the water so they can make a quick getaway.

Electricity
Electric eels are able to generate a powerful shock to stun any nearby predators.

Venom
Some creatures can deliver deadly venom to predators using fangs, spines, or tentacles.

Special features

Deadly lure
Anglerfish lure prey toward them using a special light on a rod near their mouth.

Glow
Big-fin reef squid can glow so brightly that they are visible from huge distances.

Rainbow pattern
The spines on a comb jelly refract sunlight on the water to create rainbow patterns.

Glowing bacteria
Thanks to special bacteria, Hawaiian bobtail squid can produce a glowing light.

Marine biologist
Marine biologists study aquatic animals and plants, as well as their ecosystems. Almost everything we know about marine life is thanks to them.

Underwater jobs

Some jobs require people to work underwater. Often, these roles are highly specialized, and require a lot of difficult training.

Marine archaeologist
Whether it's uncovering shipwrecks or underwater statues, marine archaeologists help us understand how humans have interacted with bodies of water across the world.

Underwater construction worker

The building and maintenance of bridges and piers, and the welding of pipelines often occurs in water. Underwater construction workers must be highly trained and confident divers.

Underwater photographer

Using special equipment, underwater photographers capture images from beneath the waves, that help us understand more about underwater environments.

Underwater tour guide

Scuba divers who are familiar with the underwater environment take groups of divers through caves and coral reefs while making sure everyone stays safe.

Diving instructor

Tourists, members of the military, and scientific researchers who want to learn to scuba dive, all rely on instructors to teach them how to do it safely.

Glossary

Apparition

An unexpected sighting of someone or something—often ghostlike.

Bacteria

Tiny living things that can be found everywhere on Earth, such as inside food, soil, or the human body.

Civilization

A society where people have built a complex city or country.

Comet

An object made of dust and ice that orbits the sun or planetary body.

Current

In water, a continuous movement in one direction.

Defense mechanisms

A reaction of an animal or plant to defend itself from danger.

Derelict

Abandoned or run down.

Eclipse

When an object in space passes into the shadow of another object.

Enclave

An enclosed place that is different from its surroundings.

Erosion

The gradual wearing away of rocks due to water and weather.

Extraterrestrial

Something that is not from Earth.

First mate

The person on a ship who is second in command.

Folklore

Traditional beliefs, stories, and customs held by a specific group of people.

Glacier

Huge, thick sheets of ice that move very slowly, either down the side of a mountain or over an area of land.

Invertebrate

An animal that does not have a backbone, such as an insect, worm, jellyfish, or spider.

Landslide

A sudden movement of a large amount of earth down a hill or mountainside.

Lava

Red-hot melted rock that has erupted on the Earth's surface, such as from a volcano.

Liquefy

To make something into a liquid.

Lure

Tempt an animal or person to do something or go somewhere.

Magma

Hot, melted rock below the Earth's surface.

Malevolent

Wanting to do evil things to others.

Maritime

Relating to the sea, especially to do with those who travel by sea.

Mythology

A collection of myths (stories) relating to a specific group of people.

Phenomena

An unusual or extraordinary occurrence.

Polyps

Tiny sea creatures that make up bigger plantlike animals, such as coral.

Privateer

Someone given permission to commit piracy by a government.

Refract

When light changes direction, such as when it travels through water.

Seafarer

Somebody who travels by sea.

Sonar

Short for "Sound Navigation and Ranging," sonar is used to find the location of objects underwater.

Submersion

When something is completely covered or surrounded by liquid.

Tidal wave

A large, often destructive, wave that can be triggered by an earthquake, strong winds, or a tsunami.

Uncharted

A place not recorded on a map.

Whirlpool

A fast, rotating area of water that can suck everything near it into its center.

Index

Penguin
Random
House

Author Tamara Macfarlane
Illustrator Alessandra Fusi
Acquisitions Editor James Mitchem
US Editor Jane Perlmutter
US Senior Editor Shannon Beatty
Senior Designer Elle Ward
Project Art Editor Jacob Da'Costa
Editor Becca Arlington
Production Editor Abi Maxwell
Senior Production Controller Ena Matagic
Jacket Co-ordinator Issy Walsh
Senior Jacket Designer Elle Ward
Deputy Art Director Mabel Chan
Publishing Director Sarah Larter

First American Edition, 2022
Published in the United States by DK Publishing
1745 Broadway, 20th Floor, New York, NY 10019

Published in Great Britain by Dorling Kindersley Limited.

A catalog record for this book
is available from the Library of Congress.
ISBN: 978-0-7440-5984-7

DK books are available at special discounts when purchased in bulk
for sales promotions, premiums, fund-raising, or educational use.
For details, contact: DK Publishing Special Markets,
1745 Broadway, 20th Floor, New York, NY 10019
SpecialSales@dk.com

Printed and bound in UAE

For the curious
www.dk.com

For Lily and Xander, my world...

The author would like to thank:
James Mitchem and the rest of the brilliant team at DK,
Alessandra Fusi for the constant joy of seeing each
beautiful new page materialize, Jennifer F. Mckinnon,
PhD, Associate Professor in the Program in Maritime
Studies for pointing me to the most exciting
underwater places, Dr. Rebecca Klaus for invoking a
passion for underwater worlds in me, Roy for every
second of listening/reading/reducing, Lils for last
minute rescue support, and the lovely Lochy Mulligan
for an endless depth of knowledge about marine life.

The publisher would like to thank:
Rea Pikula for editorial assistance, Lynne Murray
for picture library assistance, Abi Sparrow
of SP Agency, and Tamara, Jake, Ale, and
the rest of team Underwater World for
all their hard work on this project.